SUPER-CHARGED!

RADIO-CONTROLLED MODEL AIRPLANES

BY

Suzanne Lord

EDITED BY

Michael E. Goodman

PUBLISHED BY

CRESTWOOD HOUSE

Mankato, MN, U.S.A.

CIP

LIBRARY OF CONGRESS CATALOGING IN PUBLICATION DATA

Lord, Suzanne
  Radio-controlled model airplanes

  (Super-charged!)
  Includes index.
  SUMMARY: Describes the hobby of building and flying radio-controlled model airplanes. Discusses tools needed, organizations to join, and basic safety rules.
  1. Airplanes—Models—Radio control—Juvenile literature. [1. Airplanes—Models—Radio control.]
I. Goodman, Michael E. II. Title.
TL770.L58   1988   629.133'134—dc19   88-7109
ISBN 0-89686-378-6

International Standard Book Number:	Library of Congress Catalog Card Number:
0-89686-378-6	88-7109

PHOTO CREDITS

Cover: Eric Hylan
John Krekelberg: 4, 9, 11, 14, 35, 36-37, 43
Eric Hylan: 6, 20, 23
Joan Wallner: 38-39
Focus West: (Kirk Schlea) 24, 29
FPG International: (Banus March) 25; (Michael L. Valeri) 27; (J. Sylvester) 31
Sports Illustrated: (R.S. Beck) 13, 17, 32-33

Produced by Carnival Enterprises.

CRESTWOOD HOUSE

Box 3427, Mankato, MN, U.S.A. 56002

TABLE OF CONTENTS

SUPER-CHARGED!

CRESTWOOD HOUSE

A NEW HOBBY TAKES OFF

"Come on, Chris," Beth suggested. "Let's go meet the new kid."

Beth got to the new family's front door first and rang the doorbell. The new girl opened the door.

"Hi," Beth said. "My name's Beth. This is Chris. We're all neighbors now. We were going to the park. Would you like to come with us?"

The girl smiled. "I'm Jennifer," she said. "I'd really like to go with you, but I'm kind of in the middle of something right now. Would you like to

A radio-controlled model airplane requires a lot of equipment.

come in?"

"Sure!" Beth cried, pulling Chris in after her. Jennifer led them to her workroom.

"Wow," breathed Chris. "What's all this?"

Jennifer sat at a worktable scattered with pieces of wood, tubes of glue, model paint, tweezers, pliers, and other hardware tools. There were tiny engine parts and transmitter boxes in various places. And hanging from the ceiling were more model airplanes than Chris or Beth had ever seen!

"Sorry," Jennifer said. "I know the place looks pretty messy. I'm in the middle of building a model airplane. My family and I fly radio-controlled aircraft."

"What's a radio-controlled aircraft?" Chris asked.

"That's a plane that you operate in the air by sending radio wave signals to it," Jennifer said. "Why don't I show you, instead of just telling you about it?"

Beth poked Chris in the ribs. "I think we're going to like our new neighbor," she whispered.

THE HISTORY OF RADIO-CONTROLLED FLYING

For about 50 years, people have been building and flying radio-controlled (RC) aircraft. At first the

A hobbyist carries his model to the runway for its first flight.

military used full-sized, radio-controlled aircraft as targets for target practice. After awhile, someone thought of flying smaller, model planes by radio control. But the hobby had a hard time getting off the ground.

Early radio-controlled planes were heavy, hard to control, and very expensive. The first contest for radio-controlled model airplanes was held in 1936 — and no one entered! The following year, six brave "flyers" showed up. Only three of the planes actually got off the ground. And of those three, only one operator could prove that he had any "control" over what his craft was doing. He won.

During World War II, the military once again used full-sized, radio-controlled aircraft. Unmanned radio-controlled planes were equipped with cameras to take pictures behind enemy lines. Known as "flying bombs," radio-controlled aircraft packed with explosives were sent to destroy enemy targets. Back home, model airplane building was getting a big boost. The government encouraged people to build models of enemy planes so that citizens and soldiers alike would learn to recognize them.

After the war, radio-controlled flying and model airplanes teamed as many model builders became interested in the hobby. The first model radio-controlled planes were still heavy—30 pounds (14 kilograms) was an average weight! The hobby was still expensive, and operators had to get an FCC radio license from the government to operate their craft. Still, more and more people flew radio-controlled planes. The number of clubs increased, too.

In the 1960s and 1970s, RC aircraft changed. Lightweight plastics led to lighter planes. Tiny transistorized parts and new electronics led to the development of smaller, lighter, and better engines and radio-control boxes. The new planes weighed ten pounds (4 kilograms) or even less! They were also sturdier, easier to control, and far less expensive than their ancestors.

In 1983 the government changed some federal regulations that seemed "excessive." One of the regulations eliminated was the requirement of an FCC radio operator's license to operate a radio-controlled aircraft. Remember this when reading books or articles written before 1983. They may say that the license is required, but it no longer is!

Today the sport has become more popular along with other radio-controlled sports. Running radio-controlled cars is a lot of fun, and a pond filled with radio-controlled boats is a beautiful sight. But sending an actual plane into the air—a plane that you built—is a very special thrill.

INVITATION TO AN ADVENTURE

"How'd you get into this?" Chris asked Jennifer.

Jennifer laughed. "I guess I sort of grew into it," she said. "Dad started it first, and when he married Mom, she took it up. When I got old enough, they let me help. Now I can do most things for myself."

"How do you get all these little parts together?" Beth asked.

"Do you have to cut out all the pieces?" Chris asked.

"Do you make the engines, too?" Beth interrupted.

"Whoa!" Jennifer laughed. "That's too many questions at one time! Hey, I've got an idea. My family is going to a radio-control club meet next week. I'll ask if you can come along. That is, if you want to."

"Want to?" Beth exclaimed, looking at Chris.

"Just try to stop us!" Chris added.

Before each flight, radio-controlled model airplanes are carefully inspected.

THE MODEL AIRPLANE KIT

There may be as many different kinds of model planes as there are people to build them!

Most planes come in kits. Beginners use an ARF kit. ARF stands for "almost ready to fly." Parts are cut to fit and can be put together with special quick-drying glue.

RC hobbyists build and repair models all the time. An expert may be able to put together a model using only a single-edged razor blade, regular and Phillips head screwdrivers, and pliers. But most people need some extra tools and equipment.

The following tools have been suggested by expert model builders and are available in any hardware store: a small hammer for nailing in temporary "holding" pins; a model building, or "coping" saw, a jigsaw, and a hacksaw; needlenose, electrician's (insulated), and diagonal cutting pliers; an electric drill; a soldering iron; a sander or sanding block and sandpaper; a planing tool for shaping wood evenly; files for trimming wood and plastic; clamps and a medium-sized vise for holding and bending model parts; a small, sharp knife or blade for precise cutting of thin wood; an awl; and wire (ask for piano wire).

Other materials used in model building and finishing are: extra-fast-drying celluloid cement, epoxy, and white

Model airplanes are built in many sizes and colors.

11

glue; materials to go over the bare "skeleton" of a model—Japanese tissue, silkspan, silk, nylon, fiberglass cloth, or coverings that are heat shrinkable (ask your hobby store about purchasing these materials); and paints for the finished product—brushed or sprayed model "dope," epoxy paints, enamels, or polyurethane spray paints (model paint is not very expensive; it's usually less than $10).

A beginner should start with a simple ARF kit. The best ARF kits are "high wing" planes. This means that the wings are set near the top of the body of the aircraft. The wings on these planes are also larger in proportion to the body of the plane than a more advanced model. A larger wing span ensures more air cushioning for the plane. Because the weight of the "high wing" aircraft is mainly under the wing, the craft has more stability.

The model should be lightweight and have a three-wheeled "tricycle" landing gear. This type of gear has the normal two wheels, plus a "nosewheel." Launchings and landings are difficult enough for beginners—why make it more difficult by adding balance problems? The tricycle gear makes a "tail-dragging" take off or "nose first" landing less likely.

If possible, look through the instructions before purchasing the kit. They should be easy to understand. Most important, a beginner's model kit should not be expensive. An ARF kit is commonly used for training and experimentation. Once it's built, it will go through lots of rugged use as the beginner learns to take off, fly, and land the airplane. Once the beginner has the knack of flying, he or she can move onto a more advanced (and more expensive) model!

Building a model airplane takes time and patience!

THE ENGINE

Except for gliders, an engine is needed to get any model airplane flying, whether it's radio-controlled or not. Most kits don't include an engine—and there are usually many types to choose from at a hobby store. So what kind is needed? There are diesel, two- or four-cycle, electric, spark- or glow-ignition, and Wankel engines. And what size? Some engines are

A model of the Clipped Wing Cub airplane.

heavier, more powerful, or more expensive.

Diesel engines, Wankels, and engines powered by spark plugs are no longer common in RC flying. Hobbyists today prefer a two-cycle or four-cycle glow-ignition engine. Two-cycle engines have two strokes of combustion per cycle, and four-cycle have four. Four-cycle engines make less noise but are twice as expensive as two-cycle engines. They also have a lower "power-to-weight" ratio and a reputation for backfiring when starting up, which could be dangerous.

Glow-plug engines contain a wire coil hot enough

to ignite the charge in the engine's cylinder. To start the ignition, the hobbyist must connect the battery to the glow-plug and rotate the plane's propeller counterclockwise, with a "starter cone" or a "chicken stick." A hobbyist never uses bare fingers to rotate a propeller (once an airplane's propeller has started turning, its blades are sharp enough to severely injure a hobbyist's fingers and hand). After the engine is started, combustion heat keeps the coil hot and the engine's battery can be disconnected.

Glow-plug engines use their own special fuel, which can be ignited without a spark. This fuel is available at hobby stores, and is pre-mixed for model aircraft.

Electric engines are very inexpensive (from $15 to $35) as opposed to two-cycle ($35 to $100) or four-cycle ($100 to $200) engines. Electric engines also burn clean and last longer than conventional model engines. Their disadvantage is that they often cannot get a model up to the speed it needs for take off.

The instructions in a model kit should indicate what size motor is needed. Generally, the size of an engine is determined by the size and weight of the object it must move. A bigger or heavier model aircraft will need a more powerful engine.

Another factor that determines engine size is whether the plane will be taking off from concrete or grass. A plane must attain a certain speed before it can take to the air. Grass presents more friction and resistance to the plane, so a more powerful engine is needed. A less powerful engine is needed for a plane taking off from smooth concrete.

The best thing for a beginner is to talk with an experienced hobbyist about engine sizes. Radio-controlled aircraft club members or hobby shop owners can determine what size engine is right for the model being used.

RADIO CONTROL UNITS

Once the model is built and painted and the engine is added, it still needs controls to make it fly in certain directions. It's time for the radio transmitter, receiver, and "servo" motor.

The transmitter and receiver are powered by rechargeable batteries. The radio transmitter sends out a radio signal. This signal is picked up by the receiver mounted on the plane's fuselage. The receiver uses the transmitter signals to control pushrods in the "servo" motor. The pushrods operate various parts of the model plane.

The pushrods operate the rudder, or fin, mounted on the back of the plane. The rudder is the vertical piece of wood or plastic that controls the plane's side-to-side movement. When the operator moves his control switch to the left, the pushrods "steer" the plane to the left. Other pushrods are connected to the

A model airplane's control unit uses radio signals to fly the plane.

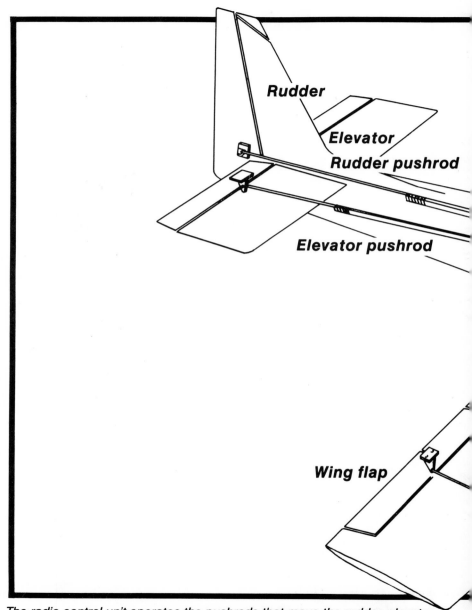

Rudder

Elevator

Rudder pushrod

Elevator pushrod

Wing flap

The radio control unit operates the pushrods that move the rudder, elevator, and wing flaps.

18

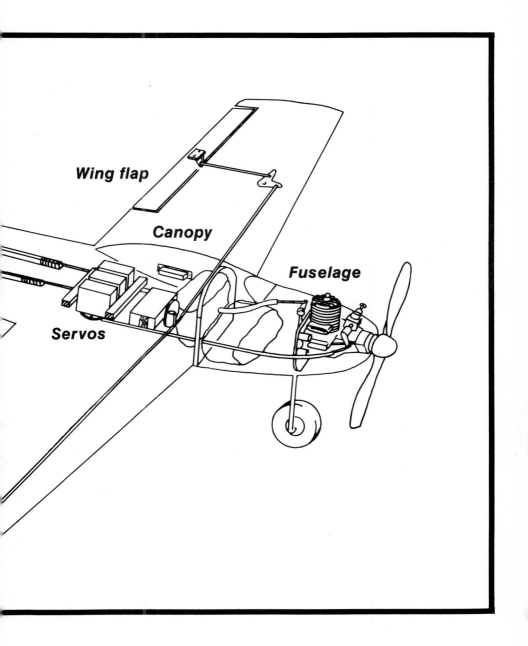

Wing flap

Canopy

Fuselage

Servos

A model of the Navy's T-28C Trojan.

elevator. The elevator is the horizontal piece of wood or plastic also mounted to the back of the plane. The elevator controls the up-and-down movement of the plane. When the operator moves the elevator pushrods up, the tail of the model airplane drops and the nose flies upward.

Some model planes are large enough to have wing flaps. These flaps are important for taking off and landing the airplane. For take off, the plane needs lift from the wind, so the flaps are down.

Many of the same types of equipment needed to fly a full-size plane are needed to fly a model radio-controlled plane!

KISS

When buying a radio controlled plane, engine, or radio control unit, "KISS" is one of the main rules. But it doesn't have anything to do with romance. It stands for "Keep it simple, silly!"

An expensive, complicated craft is a waste of time, energy, and money unless an operator is an experienced flyer. To learn the basics of flying a model airplane, a beginner should start with a model that operates the rudder and elevator only. As a flyer gains experience, he or she can move on to radio control units with more functions. Remember — KISS!

HAVING A FIELD DAY

At last the day came that Chris and Beth had been waiting for. Jennifer and her parents were taking them to a radio-controlled flying club field!

"The field in this area is pretty far away," Jennifer's dad said. "But it's big and well kept, and it's away from wires and highways."

"I see why you don't want your planes around wires," Chris said. "But what's the matter with highways?"

"Radio control transmitter signals travel on radio waves," Jennifer's mom explained. "Some of the frequencies we use can be interfered with. For example, a truck using a CB radio might cause someone to lose control of a plane."

"Everyone doesn't use the same frequency, though," Jennifer said. "There are about 18 different frequencies."

Soon they reached the field. Beth noticed the lines of people right away.

"We take turns flying," Jennifer explained. "That way there aren't too many planes up at once."

Chris noticed a pole with different colored clips on it.

"The color of each clip stands for a certain radio frequency," Jennifer's dad said. "That way each radio control flyer can see who's using which frequency on his or her radio transmitter."

"Why do you have to know that?" asked Chris.

"Because if two airplanes are using the same frequency for their signals, they could pick up one another's signals."

"And after that, they get to pick up the pieces of their models!" Jennifer joked.

Jennifer's mom and dad got to work unpacking the plane they wanted to fly that day.

"We made the box for it," Jennifer told Beth. "That way we can get it around without worrying about breaking a wing in the car. Some flyers have built planes with a six-foot (1.8-meter) wing span! These planes have detachable wings for easier transportation."

Chris looked around excitedly. "There sure are a lot of different kinds of planes," he exclaimed.

Many radio-controlled airplanes are replicas of World War II aircraft.

PROPS, GLIDERS, AND COPTERS

There are always several different types of radio-controlled aircraft at a club field.

By far the most common types of models are ones that fly with propellers. Many of these models are replicas of planes flown in World War II, or of biplanes from early air history.

Once a glider is launched, the hobbyist uses the radio controls to keep it flying.

Radio-controlled helicopters are just as much fun as model airplanes—but they need more skill.

Gliders (motorless models) are also popular. Gliders are made from the same basic materials as other RC model aircraft but are launched by hand. The radio controls allow the gliders to take advantage of air currents or warm air "lifts." Experienced operators can keep radio-controlled gliders aloft for hours at a time.

Radio-controlled helicopters are for the experienced flyer. Because they have both a main rotor and a tail rotor, RC helicopters are hard to handle. Even so, they are fascinating to watch. A radio-controlled helicopter can hover just like the real thing!

PRACTICE MAKES PERFECT—SOMETIMES

"Jennifer, it's going to be a while before we take the plane up," her mom said. "Why don't you take Chris and Beth to the beginner's field?"

Chris and Beth followed Jennifer to an out-of-the-way area where they saw a strange sight. A couple of people were walking their airplanes on the ground—like a dog on a leash!

"Why are they doing that?" Beth asked.

"They are just starting out using their controls. The airplane is on a 'leash' for safety—just in case. Also, the wings have been taken off, so the model doesn't accidentally get airborne.

"Radio-controlled planes can be dangerous," Jennifer went on. "Some models can get pretty big, and they travel 40 miles (64 kilometers) an hour or more in the air. People can get seriously hurt if they're hit by a low-flying or crashing plane. That's why club members are so careful. And that's also why everyone out here carries insurance—just in case someone gets hurt."

"Come on," Chris insisted. "There are just a couple of controls on this guy's transmitter. It looks

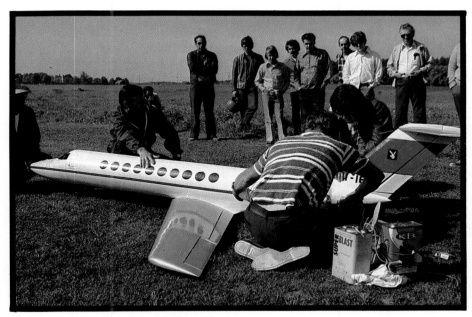

Model airplanes can be enormous!

pretty easy to me."

Jennifer smiled. "It looked that way to me, too. Then I tried it. Everything was fine as long as the plane was going away from me. Pushing the rudder lever to the left made the plane go left. No problem, right?"

"Right!" Chris and Beth echoed together.

"Wrong! When I turned the plane around and made it come back to me, I had to reverse everything! It's like a mirror image. Now I had to remember that pushing the lever to the left would send my plane to the right!"

"Hmmm," Chris decided. "Maybe it's not so simple."

THE BUDDY SYSTEM

"Look over there," Jennifer cried. "Someone's learning to take a plane up."

"Wait a minute," Beth said. "There are two people and two transmitter boxes. Who's guiding the plane?"

"They both are. One of those people is a trainer. He has a 'buddy box.' It's like the dual steering wheel in a Driver's Ed car used to train new drivers. As long as the beginner is doing okay, he controls the craft. But if something goes wrong, the trainer can take over."

The three friends watched the new flyer try to get his model plane airborne. At last he succeeded. The trainer carefully guided him step by step through a flight pattern.

"When I first started," Jennifer said, "my trainer told me, 'Don't worry about crashing your model. You will!' He was right."

"Why?" asked Chris.

"There's a lot to know and it's hard to think when your plane is in the air," explained Beth. "Once I thought my plane was flying just fine. I set the elevator flaps to make the plane go up. And instead, it shot towards the ground! Then I realized it had

28

It takes practice to successfully fly a radio-controlled model airplane.

been flying upside down!"

"You mean you can't tell from looking whether your plane is upside down or not?" Beth asked, amazed.

"Not from a distance. Remember, you're not in the plane to see where it's going. The outline of a plane turning left is pretty much the same as one going right. After a few maneuvers, you can get very confused as to what position your plane is in. Sometimes you can't tell whether your plane is going away from you or coming towards you!"

"Sounds confusing," said Chris. "How do you handle all this?"

"Verrrrrry carefully," Jennifer joked. "Anyway,

that's why beginners train on inexpensive models. That way, they don't have to worry about ruining an expensive model!"

UP, UP AND AWAAAAY!

Just then Jennifer's parents called. It was time for them to launch their plane!

"Dad's taking his favorite up today," Jennifer said proudly. "You may get to see some fancy stuff."

"I think I've worked out a nice set of maneuvers," Jennifer's dad said. "You'll see a little bit of everything."

Beth and Chris watched in awe as the plane performed all kinds of stunts—it looped, rolled, dove, pulled out, and then formed squares, figure eights, and spirals in the air.

Finally, Jennifer's dad brought the plane in. It landed perfectly.

"My heart is pounding," Chris said breathlessly. "I feel like I was up there myself!"

CLUB MEETS AND COMPETITIONS

Club competitions are usually held through permission of the Acadamy of Model Aeronautics (AMA). Individual club chapters inform the AMA

At club meets and competitions, hobbyists test their building and flying skills.

of their intention of holding a competition, when it will be, and where. The AMA "sanctions" the meet (makes it official) and handles the publicity and the insurance coverage.

All meets of this type use the competition rule book of the AMA, no matter where they're held. This ensures that a flyer from South Carolina can come to a contest in Kansas and know that the rules and regulations will be identical to what he or she is used to.

There are many tests of skill at an RC aircraft meet. But the "Big Four" contests are: soaring, pylon, pattern, and scale.

In the soaring competition, "pilots" use all their skill to keep their gliders airborne.

Soaring is a glider competition. The object is to get the model airborne, keep it that way for a specific amount of time using radio control, and land inside a "landing circle." Too much time in the air is as bad

in this contest as too little. Gliders still airborne after the "target time" have points subtracted! And landing inside that circle can be very difficult.

Pylon racing is a clocked speed race. Each craft races ten times around two pylons set at opposite ends of the flying field. The plane that races around them the fastest wins. Some aircraft have traveled over 200 miles (322 km) per hour around the pylons!

The pattern competition tests the hobbyist's flying skills. He or she must execute specific aerobatic maneuvers according to very precise standards. Before a contest, hobbyists spend many hours practicing the loops, twists, and rolls that make up the pattern competition. This part of the contest is a lot like figure skating competition in which the most perfect figure eight wins. Pattern competition has been called "figure skating in the sky."

Scale judging is a test of how closely modelers have duplicated "the real thing." Replica models are judged on how perfectly they are built "to scale." This means if a Sopwith Camel model is 1/10 scale, every part of the craft must be 1/10 the size of a real Sopwith part!

Scale judges are usually experienced model builders. Before the competition, hobbyists give each judge a photograph of the aircraft they have duplicated. The models are lined-up on the field and the judging begins. Contest judges must stand several feet away as they compare the photographs with the models. Points are given for the quality of the work and for how closely the model matches the real aircraft. Some model builders "decorate" their

Before scale judging begins, model airplanes are lined-up for inspection.

aircraft with bullet holes and smoke to duplicate a war-worn aircraft. Others paint tiny instrument panels inside the plane or add small, detailed fighter pilots.

But there's more to scale judging than just looks. A replica must be capable of doing everything its "parent" plane can do—at scale. That Sopwith replica must do 1/10 the speed, 1/10 the altitude, and all the maneuvers that the real plane could do!

There are other types of contests—although they are not all encouraged by the AMA. Mock battles are sometimes held between flyers. These contests are

Hobbyists add water skis so their model planes can land and take off on water...

potentially dangerous because, if an accident occurs, there's no place for an injured plane to go but down — possibly into a crowd of spectators. There are other safer ways to have "battles" than to destroy one another's models! In one type of combat each plane has a long ribbon attached to its tail. The plane that cuts the ribbon off the other plane is declared the

winner.

Many radio control hobbyists attend meets without entering any contests. Most simply enjoy seeing each other's models, picking up new modeling or flying tips, checking out products firsthand, watching exhibit flights, and "talking shop" with other RC aircraft hobbyists.

…and sometimes snow skis are put on so the airplane can land and take off on a snow-covered runway.

FRIENDS WITH A FLYING START

"It's time to go," Jennifer's mom announced. The model plane was carefully packed back in its box, and everyone piled into the car. Everyone had a good time—and a whole new world had opened up for Beth and Chris!

"Would you mind very much," Chris asked, "if I watched you make models? I'd like to know more about radio-controlled aircraft."

"Me, too," Beth added. "We'd be really careful, and we'd be really quiet."

"I'd love for you to come over!" Jennifer said. "But you'd better not be quiet—I expect lots and lots of questions. One of the best parts of any hobby is sharing it!"

"Hey," Beth said to Chris. "Why are you grinning like that?"

"I was just thinking," Chris answered. "You and I have always been the Dynamic Duo, Beth. But I think the Terrific Trio just got its start!"

POINTS TO PONDER

The hobby of radio-controlled model airplanes can be fun, exciting, and challenging—but it can also be hard work! A hobbyist must like building models and tinkering with engines.

A builder must be patient. A hobbyist who can't stand to fail at things is going to be angry a lot! There can be frustration in getting any model just right. And in the beginning, there'll be many awkward flights and undoubtedly a crash or two. Anyone who quits right away if things don't go right ought to think again before getting into RC aircraft!

Transportation is an important consideration. How is the hobbyist going to get him or herself and the model to the local flying field? It's great to have a radio-controlled craft, but it won't be much fun if it sits in the basement!

Probably the most important question is: how responsible is the person who is considering RC flying as a hobby? Safety is important in flying radio-controlled aircraft. It's a hobby to learn step by step, and there's no room for "hotshotting."

STARTING YOUR NEW HOBBY

If radio-controlled flying is for you, the first step is to do a lot of reading about the subject. You might start out at the library. Any one of several books written about the subject may be available in the "Hobby" section.

Visit your local hobby shop, too. The people there will either have literature on the subject or know how to order it. A hobby shop will also have the latest issue of a magazine called *RC Modeler.* This magazine is a must for the new hobbyist. Another good magazine to look through is *Model Builder. Model Builder* magazine writes about all sorts of model airplanes—but radio-controlled models get a good deal of attention.

In addition to magazines, there are several good books written by experts in the RC aircraft field. These books can be found at your local hobby shop.

Most books include step-by-step instructions for all aspects of model building and flying. Many offer very helpful pictures and charts. Other books include first-hand accounts of the experts' own trials as beginners—and tell helpful hints to aid the beginning hobbyist over potential rough spots.

Some books specialize in one area of RC flying. There are, for instance, books only about RC gliders. Other books include all RC sports, such as boating and cars, with aircraft occupying only a part of the pages.

Although they may be costly, buyer's guides to RC flying can be a good purchase. Buyer's guides contain very complete listings of models and all the equipment needed for the RC aircraft hobbyist. And of course, these guides list one very important item to the hobbyist—price lists!

An experienced hobbyist can build and paint an elaborate radio-controlled model airplane.

43

ORGANIZATIONS

The most important step for an RC airplane hobbyist is to join the Academy of Model Aeronautics. It's the nerve center for almost every radio control flying club.

AMA members receive a listing of clubs in their area. They receive regular issues of *RC Modeler* magazine. The AMA sponsors many meets and competitions. And members are automatically covered with a $1 million liability insurance policy, in case of injuries as a result of an RC flying accident.

If you want to know more about radio-controlled gliders, you can contact the League of Silent Flight, an international organization. Or you can join the National Soaring Society. The National Soaring Society sponsors local and national gliding meets and entitles members to monthly issues of *Sailplane* magazine.

Radio-controlled airplanes, gliders, and helicopters provide a lot of fun for the person who likes to build models, tinker with engines and radio controls, and fly. If you are able to, attend a club meet in your area. It's a great place for a new RC flyer to see what this hobby is all about. Like Beth and Chris, you may find a whole new world of adventure opening up for you!

FOR MORE INFORMATION

For more information about buying, building, and flying radio-controlled airplanes and gliders, write to:

The Academy of Model Aeronautics
1810 Samuel Morse Drive
Reston, VA 22090

League of Silent Flight
P.O. Box 647
Mundelein, IL 60060

The National Soaring Society
3755 Berkley Lane
Lumberton, NC 28358

GLOSSARY/INDEX

AEROBATICS 34 — *Flying tricks not used in normal flight.*

AIR CURRENTS 25 — *Wind directions which affect aircraft.*

ARF KIT 10, 12 — *Partially constructed ("almost ready to fly") model airplane kits.*

BIPLANE 23 — *An airplane with two sets of wings, one on top of the other.*

BUDDY BOX 28 — *Dual-control radio control transmitters for a trainer and beginning RC pilot.*

ELEVATOR FLAPS 20, 21, 28 — *Horizontal tail assembly parts that control the up and down motion of an aircraft.*

FCC 7, 8 — *Federal Communications Commission, a government group that regulates radio and television activities.*

FLIGHT PATTERN 28 — *A set of precise flying maneuvers.*

FUSELAGE 16 — *The body of an aircraft.*

GLIDER 13, 25, 32, 33, 42, 44, 45 — *A motorless airplane that flies on air currents.*

HIGH WING PLANE 12 — *A plane whose wings attach higher on the body of the plane than usual.*

HOTSHOTTING 41 — *Trying more complicated maneuvers than one can safely handle; showing off.*

LIABILITY INSURANCE 44 — *Protection against being responsible for paying for injuries caused in an RC aircraft flying accident.*

GLOSSARY / INDEX

PUSHRODS 16, 20 — *Rods connecting the servo motor to the parts of the model plane that they will move.*

RADIO FREQUENCY 21, 22 — *Radio wave signals sent from a transmitter on the ground to a receiver on a model plane.*

RECEIVER 16 — *Part of an RC unit that receives the radio signals sent from the transmitter.*

RUDDER 16, 21, 27 — *The vertical part of a plane, located at the rear, that controls left and right motion.*

SERVO MOTOR 16 — *A small electric motor outfitted with rods which move various parts of a radio-controlled aircraft in response to signals from the ground transmitter.*

TRAINING MODEL 28 — *Sturdy, easy to handle equipment for beginning hobbyists.*

TRANSMITTER 5, 16, 21, 22, 26, 28 — *Part of a radio control unit which sends radio signals to a radio control receiver mounted on the aircraft.*

TRANSISTORS 7 — *Miniature electrical parts.*

TRICYCLE LANDING GEAR 12 — *Three-wheeled landing gear for an aircraft.*

UP/DOWN DRAFTS — *Up- or down-wind currents which affect aircraft.*

WARM AIR LIFTS 25 — *Warm air rising, giving a "lift" to aircraft passing through it.*